DEAR
FATHER
IN
HEAVEN

DEAR FATHER IN HEAVEN

Prayers for Boys and Girls
written and compiled by
Robert H. Schlesselman and
Luella Spitzack Ahrens

Concordia Publishing House
Saint Louis, Missouri

Concordia Publishing House, Saint Louis 18, Missouri

Concordia Publishing House, Ltd., London, W.C. 1.

Copyright 1963 by Concordia Publishing House

Library of Congress Catalog Card No. 62-19956

INTRODUCTION

Dear Friend of God:

This is a special book just for you. It can be one of the most exciting books you will ever use. It can help you *talk to God!*

Why talk to God? Because He is your Father—your Father in heaven—and children always talk to their father. "You are all the children of God through faith in Christ Jesus," God promises you in His Word (Galatians 3:26). Pretty wonderful, isn't it? By believing in Jesus, who died for your sins, you have become a child of the Creator and Ruler of all things! Now, just *being* a child of God is better than being a child of a president or king. But actually *talking* to God is more thrilling and helpful and joyful than talking to a president or our earthly parents or our closest friends.

You will notice that many of the talks or prayers in this book close with the word "for Jesus' sake," or words like those. We can pray to our heavenly Father because of Jesus and His work on earth. Through Jesus we know and love the true God. The salvation which Jesus won for us on the cross gives us a clean heart and a new spirit with which we go to God in prayer.

The Holy Spirit also has a part in prayer. Since we

are the children of God, the Spirit lives in our hearts and makes us want to pray. Always be ready to listen to Him!

As you use the prayers in this book, you will notice that there are different kinds of prayers—in fact, there are five kinds. There are things you will want to ask God for and things you'll want to thank Him for. There will be times when you will want to ask Him to help others and times when you'll want to admit your wrongs to Him. And finally, there will be the times when you just want to tell Him how much you love Him — just because He *is* your Father, your Savior, your Helper, your God. These five kinds of prayer are called: petition (asking), Matthew 7:7; thanksgiving, Ephesians 5:20; intercession (asking God to help others), Matthew 15:22-28; confession (admitting your sins), Luke 18:13; adoration or praise, Psalm 100. Perhaps you will want to find and read the passages listed here for each of them.

You will find all five of these kinds of "talks with God" in this book. In many prayers you will find more than one kind. Let these prayers be a start for you, but then pray more "on your own." Never let these be the only prayers you use. Perhaps these will give you some ideas about how you can pray just from your own heart.

In the last two units of the book you will find a short Bible reading listed with each prayer topic. These are given to help you have a more complete talk with God. Not only will you be talking to Him but He will be talking to you also. Through His Word and the work of the Holy Spirit your faith becomes stronger and you will have the power to be a better Christian.

Your prayer life means much to you—and to God.

Just think how often you talk to your parents. How much more important and also how natural it is for a son or daughter to speak with Him. You know, the apostle Paul tells us to "pray without ceasing," 1 Thess. 5:17. Make your life a life of constant prayer and worship. Keep a prayer on your lips and heart all through each day. If this little book helps you do just that, Jesus will be happy, and you will be a true child of God.

May the Lord bless you as you learn how to pray.

Your friends in Christ,

Robert H. Schlesselman
Luella Spitzack Ahrens

CONTENTS

CONTENTS

Be with me in work and in play,
In all that I do and in all that I say.

MORNING
AND
EVENING
PRAYERS

Sunday Morning

O heavenly Father, give me Your Holy Spirit in Sunday school and church so that I may really worship You with all my heart. Thank You for letting me worship together with many other people who love You. Amen.

In Your holy name, O Lord, I begin this new week. I ask You to be with me as I go to church, that all I hear may lead me to love You more and may help me to lead a holy life. Bless our pastor and all who speak Your Word today. Send Your Spirit into the hearts of those who hear, that they may believe in Jesus as their Savior. Remind me that all who trust in You will on the Last Day live with You in heaven. In Jesus' name I pray. Amen.

Sunday Evening

At the end of this holy day, dear Father, I thank You for talking to me in Your holy Word. Help me to remember what I heard and to do Your will, through Jesus Christ. Amen.

Lord God, loving Father, You have made me Your child. Help me to show this week that I am Your child. Keep me from giving in to temptations. Lord

Jesus, remind me of how You died for me. Give me strength to live for You. Holy Spirit, stay in my heart. Help me to love people. Amen.

Monday Morning

Dear Jesus, be with me in work and in play,
In all that I do and in all that I say. Amen.

All through the day I humbly pray:
Be You my Guard and Guide;
My sins forgive, and let me live,
Blest Jesus, near Your side. Amen.

Monday Evening

I thank You for the love so true
That watched o'er me the long day through.
Dear Savior, keep me through the night,
And wake me with the morning's light. Amen.

O God, as I look back on how I lived and behaved today, I am sorry for my sins. Forgive me, and make me sure that You love me always for Jesus' sake. Keep me safe during this night that I may get up tomorrow morning and be ready for another day, through Jesus, my Lord. Amen.

Tuesday Morning

Keep me this day, dear God, from falling into sin. While I work and play, help me to remember how kind and good You are. Help me to be kind and good to others, for Jesus' sake. Amen.

Almighty God, thank You for the light of day, the air I breathe, the life I live. Help me to live this day with You and for You. I pray for Your protection for myself and for those whom I love. Bless my home so that our family may be happy in Your love. Be with all who are sick and lonely. Give me Your strength and Your salvation in Jesus, their Savior. I pray in His holy name. Amen.

Tuesday Evening

Dear Father in heaven, I thank You for night and for sleep. Watch over me and give me a rested body for work and play tomorrow, for Jesus' sake. Amen.

Heavenly Father, the light of the day has gone away, and the lights for the night have been put into the sky. As You watch over the stars, You watch also over me. I thank You for being so good to me. For Jesus' sake forgive the sins I have done today. Keep me tonight as Your child through faith in Your Son. Amen.

Wednesday Morning

Now the shades of night are gone,
Now the morning light is come.
Lord, may I be Yours today;
Drive the shades of sin away. Amen.

I thank You, my heavenly Father, through Jesus Christ, Your dear Son, that You have kept me this night from all harm and danger; and I pray You that

Thank You for the light of day,
the air I breathe, the life I live.

You would keep me this day also from sin and every evil, that all my doings and life may please You. For into Your hands I commend myself, my body and soul, and all things. Let Your holy angel be with me, that the wicked Foe may have no power over me. Amen. (Luther's Morning Prayer)

Wednesday Evening

The day is past and over;
All thanks, O Lord, to You!
I pray You now that without sin
The hours of darkness be.
O Jesus, keep me in Your sight
And keep me through the coming night. Amen.

I thank You, my heavenly Father, through Jesus Christ, Your dear Son, that You have graciously kept me this day; and I pray You that You would forgive me all my sins where I have done wrong, and graciously keep me this night. For into Your hands I commend myself, my body and soul, and all things. Let Your holy angel be with me, that the wicked Foe may have no power over me. Amen. (Luther's Evening Prayer)

Thursday Morning

O Lord, for Your keeping
While I was sleeping,
I thank You and pray,
Be with me today. Amen.

I begin another day in Your name, O Lord, Savior of all people. Thank You for all the mercies, which I do not deserve. I pray, give me faith and love and make me a living witness for You. Help me today to live and speak so that I do not bring shame to Your holy name. Bless my words and deeds that I may bring someone closer to You. And, Lord, show me how exciting and happy this day can be when I live it as Your helper. Amen.

Thursday Evening

Heavenly Father, forgive my sins of this day for Jesus' sake. Let Your angels keep me safe this night. Give me, as You have promised, Your Holy Spirit. Amen.

I come to You again tonight in my prayers, O Lord. You have told me to ask, and You have promised to hear me. You have given me food to eat, clothes to wear, air to breathe, and people to love. Help others to know and love You that they may be as happy as I am. Trusting only in You, I pray: Keep me and those whom I love through this night, for Jesus' sake. Amen.

Friday Morning

Dear Lord,
Help me to do the things I should,
To be to others kind and good
In all I do—in work and pray—
To grow more loving every day. Amen.

I thank You for this new day, most kind Savior. Keep me strong in faith this day and always. Guide me in my work and play. If trouble comes, give me kindness and patience to say and do what is pleasing to You. Give me love to forgive those who hurt me. Amen.

Friday Evening

As I go to sleep tonight, I have a good feeling because I know, dear Jesus, that You love me and are always with me. Amen.

Dear Father, You know all things I have done today. Nothing can be hidden from You. Bless all that has been good. Forgive what has been wrong, through Jesus, who saved me by His blood. As Your child I put my trust in You. Help me never to leave You. Be with me this night and also with those who are away from home and those who are sick. Hear all my prayers for Jesus' sake. Amen.

Saturday Morning

Dear God, thank You for keeping me through the night from harm and danger. Help me this last day of the week to get my heart ready to keep Your holy day. Amen.

Lord God, You have kept Your promises in the week now ending. For all of this I thank You, O Lord, and I bless Your holy name. Bless the time I have today

Keep me strong in faith this day and always.

for work and play. Help me get ready to meet You in Sunday school and church tomorrow. Make my body, mind, and soul strong to be ready for the new week. Help all of us in this home to be a blessing to one another and to many others, through the love of Jesus. Amen.

Saturday Evening

Dear Father in heaven, I thank You for all the blessings You have given me this week. As the church bells call tomorrow, make my heart ready to hear Your Word. Amen.

Loving Father, I know Your love has been with me in the week ending tonight, and I know that I have sinned many times. Forgive me. Give me Your Spirit to make me strong to live a more holy life in the week to come. Be with me as I go to church and Sunday school tomorrow. Bless the Word I will hear, and help me to obey it. Take care of me during this night for the sake of Jesus, Your Son, my Lord and Savior. Amen.

TABLE
PRAYERS

Before Meals

Feed Your children, God most holy,
Comfort sinners poor and lowly,
O You Bread of Life from heaven,
Bless the food You here have given. Amen.

You open wide Your hand, O Lord,
The earth is filled with good;
Teach us with thankful hearts to take
From You our daily food. Amen.

Come, Lord Jesus, be our Guest,
Our morning Joy, our evening Rest,
And with Your daily food impart
Your love and peace to every heart. Amen.

Returning Thanks

For all these gifts, O Lord,
Make us truly thankful. Amen.

For all Your gifts, dear God, so free,
To You we ever thankful be. Amen.

To God, who gives us daily bread,
A thankful song we'll raise,
And pray that He who sends our food
Will fill our hearts with praise. Amen.

Bless the Lord, O my soul, and all that is within me,
bless His holy name.
Bless the Lord, O my soul, and forget not all His
benefits. Amen.

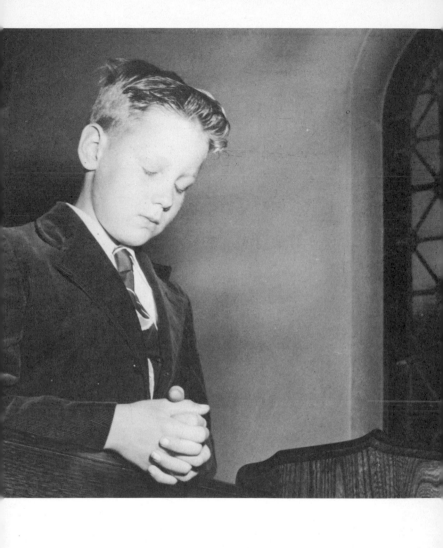

PRAYERS
IN
CHURCH

Come, very Sun of truth and love,
Come in Your radiance from above,
And shed Your Holy Spirit's ray
On all we hear, do, think, and say. Amen.

Come and meet with me today;
Teach me, Lord, Yourself, I pray. Amen.

May Your Word be a lamp unto my feet and a light
unto my path. Amen.

I thank You, heavenly Father,
For all that I have heard;
Teach me to love my Savior
And to obey Your Word. Amen.

Still on Your holy Word
Help us to feed and grow
That we may learn to know You, Lord,
And practice what we know. Amen.

Let the words of my mouth and the meditation of
my heart be acceptable in Your sight, O Lord, my
Strength and my Redeemer. Amen.

PRAYERS
OF THE
CHURCH
YEAR

Advent

Dear Lord Jesus, as the days of Christmas draw near, help me to remember that Christmas is Your birthday. As we get ready to celebrate the festival at home and in our church and to enjoy the gifts, remind us that You are God's best Christmas Gift. Come and live in our hearts with love. Amen.

Christmas

On this day of Your birth, dear Lord, I again rejoice over the wonderful news that my Savior, my King, was born. How great is Your love! Thank You for becoming a Child on earth to fulfill the Law for me and for taking away my sins. Because of Your love to me, fill me with love for others. Make me willing to share the Christmas joy, as well as all my other blessings, with those who need Your love. In Your name I pray. Amen.

New Year

Another year to walk the way
That other steps have trod,
Another year of thankfulness,
Another year with God. Amen.

Dear heavenly Father, although I have sinned many times in the past year, You have not forgotten me. You have not taken away Your gifts of food, clothing, home, school, church, and all blessings. For these I am thankful. As I begin a new year, be with me, guide me, keep me from temptation. Help me to live my life for You. Make me strong when trouble comes, and let me walk with You in the path that leads to heaven. For Jesus' sake. Amen.

Lent

Lord Jesus Christ, as I again remember Your suffering and death, I thank You for Your great love. Teach me to see how helpless I am without You. By Your Holy Spirit turn my heart to You, the only Savior. Help me to see the cause of Your suffering, and fill me with true sorrow over my sins. Give me faith to do only those things which please You. I give myself to You. Amen.

Good Friday

Dear Savior, You suffered and died because You loved me. Help me to love You forever and ever. Amen.

O Christ, Lamb of God, I come to Your cross, sorry for my sins, asking for mercy and forgiveness. My sins have added to Your suffering. You died that I might live forever. Your death heals my soul, brings peace to my mind, and cleans my heart. Help me to hate sin that I may daily walk by faith, giving myself to You. Keep me faithful to my end until I stand before Your throne to worship You. Hear my prayer, O Redeemer. Amen.

Easter

Dear Savior, on this happy Easter Day raise us from the dead life of sin as You rose from the grave. Amen.

O Lord of all, with us abide,
In this our joyful Eastertide.
Alleluia! Amen.

"This is the day which the Lord has made. We will rejoice and be glad in it. He is risen! Hallelujah!" Heavenly Father, thank You for raising Jesus from the dead. Thank You for the proof that my sins are forgiven, that I can live forever in heaven with Him in glory. Just as He rose from the dead with a holy body, give me the power to live a holy life. Help me to remember that He is always alive, always beside me, always ready to help when temptation comes. You live, O Lord! I am Your child! Thank You, Lord. Amen.

Ascension

Lord Jesus, remind me that heaven is my real home. Amen.

"*This is the day which the Lord has made.*
We will rejoice and be glad in it."

Great King of glory, today I am happy that You went to heaven, showing all the world that You are the Winner over sin, death, and the devil. You sit at the right hand of God, ruling over the world, remembering us in love. Even though I cannot see You, I know that You are with me, to lead me, to take care of me. Give me a heart that follows You, and help me to be a good example to all people. Amen.

Pentecost

Lord God, Holy Ghost, thank You for making me a child of God. Amen.

Blessed Lord Jesus, I thank You for sending the Holy Spirit into my heart. Through my Baptism You have made me one of Your children and a member of the holy Christian church. You have given me faith, but I am still weak and I sin much. Therefore send Your Spirit to make my faith stronger, and give me power to love You more. Bless the Word that is taught everywhere so that many will turn from sin and cling to You as their Savior. Amen.

Reformation

Dear God, thank You for the Holy Bible. Help me to love the Bible as the true Word of God. Amen.

Dear heavenly Father, I thank You on this special day for giving me the true Word of God and for all those who teach me the pure Gospel story. From

Your pure Word, I know I cannot be saved by my own good works. Help me to trust only in Jesus for forgiveness of all my sins and for eternal salvation. Preserve me from false teachers, who would destroy my soul. Help all people to hear the wonderful story of Your love. Grant that I may be a true and diligent student of Your Word and may lead a holy life. I ask this in the name of Jesus, who died to save me. Amen.

Thanksgiving

Dear heavenly Father, thank You for all Your gifts, and help me to use these gifts in the right way. For Jesus' sake. Amen.

I am very thankful, dear Father in heaven, that You have given me the Bible, my church, my home, my country, my friends, and all other gifts. Make me thankful every day of my life for the greatest gift, salvation through my Savior, Jesus Christ. Make me more like Him. In His name I pray. Amen.

PRAYERS
FOR
OTHERS

Family

Ephesians 6:1-4

Lord Jesus, thank You for making us a happy family. Grant that we keep on loving You and loving one another. Amen.

Lord Jesus, my Friend and Savior, remember my family in love. Help my parents to live a life that is pleasing to You, that they may lead me to love You more and more. Take care of my brothers and sisters and keep them always in Your love. Forgive us when we forget to live as Christians and make us a family with whom You are pleased to be. Amen.

Parents

John 19:25-27

Dear Father in heaven, I know that I have not always honored my father and mother. Please forgive me for Jesus' sake and open my eyes to see how through them You are showing me how to live, and how through them You take care of me and lead me closer to You. Help my parents and me to do Your will out of love for Jesus, our Savior, who died for us all. Amen.

My Home

Psalm 90

Father in heaven, from above
Look down upon our home in love,
And for Your gifts so full and free
To you we ever thankful be. Amen.

Lord Jesus, come to us and make our home a place
in which You want to live. Let the happiness of Your
Word be with us. Make our faith strong so that
when we are tempted to sin we can resist the temptation and not worry or be troubled. Give us the
things we need for body and soul and make us kind
and forgiving to one another that we may be blessed
and at last reach our home with You in heaven,
through Jesus Christ. Amen.

Friends

Proverbs 17:13-17

Dear Lord Jesus, I am thankful for my true friends,
but I would have You for my dearest Friend. Let me
love all my friends, but love You most of all. Make
me, like You, a friend of all children. Amen.

My Church

Acts 4:32-37

Great God and King, I thank You for the holy
Christian church, where all of us who have faith in
Jesus are tied together by Your love. I thank You for

calling me into Your church and making me one of Your people and an heir of heaven. Make me willing to work hard to win those who do not know Jesus so that they, too, may walk with all Christians on the way to heaven. In Jesus' name. Amen.

Pastors and Teachers
1 Thessalonians 5:12,13

Dear God, help my pastor and teachers to be wise and good. Make me kind and helpful to them. Remind me always that they are Your servants. In Jesus' name. Amen.

Dear heavenly Father, thank You for the men and women who teach Your holy Word and lead me in the way of faith and love. Fill them with Your Holy Spirit that they may understand Your Word and teach me in words I can understand. May Your love for me lead me to listen, remember, and do what the Bible teaches. Hear me for Jesus' sake. Amen.

My Sunday School Teacher
Mark 4:14-20

I thank You, O God, for the many fine Christians who lead children to Jesus by teaching Sunday school classes. I also thank You for the time my teacher gives to You and me in studying and teaching Your lessons well. Grant him (her) the right understanding of Your Word and give him (her) words that I

Let me love all my friends,
but love You most of all.

can understand. Make me and all my classmates willing to learn and willing to do what pleases You. In Jesus' name. Amen.

Missionaries

John 3:14-18

Dear Lord Jesus Christ, I pray for all the missionaries of the church—in our land and in faraway lands. Bless them, and help them in their work. Give us such love that we may help them too. Amen.

Dear Lord Jesus, we thank You for the many faithful Christians who tell the story of Your love throughout the world. Bless the Word which our missionaries speak, that all who hear will believe and trust in You. When things go hard for them, remind them that You are with them with Your power and Spirit and that their work is not in vain. Take care of them and their families and make them happy in their work. Make me a good missionary too. Amen.

Missions

Psalm 67

Dear Lord, even though I cannot preach to all the world, grant that I may do what I can. Since I want all to enjoy Your wonderful love, I pray that the Gospel may be preached in all countries and languages. Through Your Spirit kindle the light of faith in the hearts of all who hear. Bless radio and television missions and all other ways of bringing the good news of Your love to all. Amen.

Those Who Do Not Know Jesus

Acts 4:23:31

Dear Jesus, I feel very sorry for the millions of people who do not know You and do not know that only You can save them from sin. Be with our missionaries and bless their work as they tell the heathen of Your love so that they, too, may believe in You and live with You in heaven. Amen.

My Country

Deuteronomy 8:7-20

Dear God, thank You for our great country. Bless our President and all people who work for our government. Help me to love You and to be a good citizen. In Jesus' name. Amen.

I am thankful, O God, that You have made our country a great nation. You have made us a free people who can go to church and study Your Word without being afraid. You have given us good leaders and a wonderful, beautiful land. Help us to stay true to You, to follow the rules and laws of our country. In Jesus' name. Amen.

President and Leaders

1 Timothy 2:1-4

Dear Father in heaven, I pray for the President and all the officers of our country. Give them wisdom and courage to rule our land well. Fill their hearts with love for You. In Jesus' name. Amen.

Loving Father, we know that the President and other leaders of our country have great things to do. Give them the strength and wisdom to do what is right. Keep them true, honest, strong, just, and fair to all, and help all people to be law-abiding and loyal. Be with our land and grant us the blessings of righteousness, order, and peace, for Jesus' sake. Amen.

For the Sick

Hebrews 12:5-11

O dear Lord Jesus, You were kind to the sick and suffering when You lived on earth. In the same way show Your love to those who are ill today. Take away their pain and suffering, and bless whatever the doctors do to make them well. Remind them all that even sickness is for their own good, to bring them closer to You. Through Your own suffering and death You have saved us all and forgiven all our sins. Give this same comfort to the sick and, if it pleases You, heal them, for Your name's sake. Amen.

For the Handicapped

Proverbs 20:11-15

Dear Lord God, may I remember all who need Your help—the poor, the blind, the deaf, the crippled, the homeless. Grant that I may be kind to them and show them love even as You love me. Lead them to know that these trials are for some good and that comfort for all their problems may be found with

You. Teach me to be thankful always for the health with which You have blessed me. In Jesus' name. Amen.

For Those Who Are Unkind to Me
Matthew 5:43-48

Dear Jesus, I know how much You love me and forgive me even though I sin every day. May I forgive and pray for those who hurt me and are unkind to me. Help me to overcome my desire to get even, and move me to love my enemies as You loved Yours. Amen.

For Peace in the World
Matthew 5:1-9

Dear heavenly Father, how men hate and fight one another! Have mercy on them and change their hearts. Enable us, too, by Your Spirit, to be at peace and to make peace wherever we can. Help us to do this by telling people all over the world about the peace they can have with You through faith in Christ. Forgive all who have forgotten You. Remove all war and fighting. Have mercy on those who must suffer, and comfort them with Your love, through Jesus Christ, my Lord. Amen.

PRAYERS
FOR
MYSELF

When I Am Angry

Genesis 4:3-8

Dear God, please forgive me for being angry. I love Jesus, my Savior, and I want to be Your child. Help me to remember Your great love when I am tempted to be angry with anyone. Amen.

Heavenly Father, please forgive me for getting angry so easily. Keep me from losing my temper and hating others when things don't go my way. Make me loving, kind, patient, and understanding—more like Jesus. Give me a stronger faith so that I will forgive and forget when I am wronged, through Jesus Christ, my Lord. Amen.

When I Am Afraid

Psalm 23

Dear Savior, when I am in danger, help me to trust in You. Watch over me, and let me never be afraid, for You are always near. Amen.

Dear Jesus, I know that You are always with me and that I belong to You. Take away all my fears. Make me brave when danger comes. Keep me from anything that would really hurt me. Forgive me for not trusting in You enough. Strengthen my trust in You by making me sure that You love me and are my Savior. Amen.

When I Am Selfish
Luke 6:30-36

My dear Jesus, please keep me from being selfish with what I have. Help me to remember that all I have is a gift from You. Give me a heart that is willing to share these gifts with those who need help, because You freely gave Your all for me. Amen.

After I Have Quarreled
Psalm 130

Dear Lord Jesus, put Your loving Spirit into my heart that I may do good to everyone, even to those who are not fair to me. I am sorry I have quarreled. Forgive me, and make me kind and loving. Amen.

Forgive me, Lord, for losing my temper, for getting angry. I said words which I should not have said. For this I am sorry. Help me to be strong enough not to sin like this again. When I am tempted, let me see that quarreling and fighting please only the devil. I want to be Your child, dear Savior. Amen.

To Remind Me of My Baptism
Mark 16:14-16

Dear Lord Jesus, I thank You for making me Your child through Baptism. Give me grace to love and serve You always. Amen.

Through my Baptism, dear Jesus, I became Your child. I was given faith, forgiveness, and the hope of heaven. Forgive me for not always thinking of this wonderful blessing. When I am tempted to sin, when I forget that I am Your child, when I am sad, remind me that through the water of Baptism all the love and hope of God's Word was given to me. May this always make me feel happy and peaceful in You. Amen.

When I Am Tempted to Sin
Psalm 34:11-16

We are little children, weak and apt to stray;
Savior, guide and keep us in the heavenly way.
Save us, Lord, from sinning; watch us day by day;
Help us now to love You. Take our sins away. Amen.

Dear God, I know that Your love is big enough to take care of all my troubles. Forgive me when I do something that is sinful. I know that You will keep me on the right path. Make me strong to follow You, to resist all temptations. Keep me holy, as You are holy, for the sake of Jesus. Amen.

When in Trouble
Psalm 46

Dear God, help me to remember that Your love is strong enough to carry me through all my troubles. Forgive me for being afraid, and fill my heart with love and trust in You. In Jesus' name. Amen.

Remind me, dear Lord Jesus, that You are always with me and ready to help me when in trouble. Make me kind, honest, and truthful in what I do and say, and make me sorry for my sins. Let Your love show me that no trouble will be too difficult for me to suffer. With Your help I will be happy and free. Amen.

When Death Comes
1 Corinthians 15:12-22

Oh, how good is Jesus!
May He hold my hand
And at last receive me
In the heavenly land. Amen.

Father, Son, and Spirit,
Give me grace that I
Always live a Christian,
And a Christian die. Amen.

Even though I am sad, O Lord, I thank You for taking my loved one to be with You in heaven. Help me to say, "Thy will be done" and to know that when someone dies this is Your will and that on the Last Day we are going to be together in heaven because Jesus rose from the dead for us. Do not leave me alone in this sad time. Make me strong to accept what You send. In Jesus' name I ask it. Amen.

When I Am Sick
Mark 1:40-45

Dear Jesus, when You were on earth, You helped many people get well. You can help me also today. Please help me to get well and strong soon, if it is Your will. Teach me to take good care of my health. Amen.

O dear Jesus, You were kind to the sick and suffering when You were here on earth. Show me, I pray, the same kindness in my sickness. Be merciful to me and send Your help. Bless the doctor so that he will do what is good for me. If it is Your will, let me get well soon. Take away my pain and make me strong again. While I am sick, help me to patiently suffer what I must and to remember that Your suffering saved me from all sins. For Your name's sake I ask it. Amen.

To Understand His Word
John 6:60-69

Teach me, O Lord, to love Your Book and to understand it. Bless all the people who teach me Your holy Word, and make me able and ready to tell many others of Your great love in Jesus. Amen.

*Please help me to get well
and strong soon.*

Your Word, the Bible, dear God, was written that we might know the way to heaven — faith in Jesus. Send the Holy Spirit into my heart that I may learn to know better and better that Jesus is my Savior and that He makes me able to lead a Christian life. Bless my parents, my pastor, and all who teach me Your Word, and grant them wisdom to speak Your message in words that children can understand. In Jesus' name I ask it. Amen.

For Stronger Faith

Hebrews 11:8-16

Give me a heart, dear Jesus, filled with so much love for You that I can serve You gladly and worship You sincerely. Amen.

Dear Father in heaven, I want to keep on growing as a Christian. Send Your Spirit into my heart to make my faith stronger. Teach me more about Jesus, my Savior, that when I am tempted to sin I can resist the devil. Forgive my lack of trust. I know You will never leave me, because I am Yours in Jesus. Amen.

For Forgiveness

Psalm 51:1-9

Forgive me where I have this day
Done some wrong in work or play;
Oh, help me always do what's right
And bless me every day and night! Amen.

Dear Lord Jesus, please forgive all the wrongs I have done. Take away all my sins, which are like a heavy load. I know You can, because You are God's Son and have the power to forgive sins. I am sorry that with my sins I caused Your death, but I am thankful, Jesus, that You freed me with Your blood. Amen.

To Use My Gifts

Psalm 50:10-15

Dear Father, You loved me so much that You gave Your own Son for me. Impress this loving-kindness on my heart that I may be always thankful for all You have given me. Help me to use my gifts in serving others. Amen.

Dear heavenly Father, all things in heaven and earth belong to You and I really don't own anything. Make me willing to use in ways that please You what You have given me. Keep me from being selfish and greedy. Make me thankful for the money and things You have given me and willing to share them with others, for Jesus' sake. Amen.

For An Understanding Heart

Psalm 51:10-12

Guard me from sin, my hand Thou take;
Lord Jesus, Thou my heart do make
A home for You until I see
The heavenly home prepared for me. Amen.

Dear Father, sometimes I want to ask, Why must I be good? Why can't I have my way? Why must I work and study hard? Oh, therefore, help me to understand that You have a plan for my life. Let me believe that everything fits together and works for my good. Open my heart to know Your will that I may love and trust You more, for Jesus' sake. Amen.

To Know Jesus
John 14:1-6

Lord Jesus, help me to love You more and more and to serve and worship You with all my heart as my Savior from sin. Amen.

Dear Father in heaven, we can never thank You enough for sending Your Son Jesus to this earth to save us from all sin. Grant that I may know Him, not just as a great man and a good teacher but as Your very Son, my Savior and Redeemer, who suffered and died and rose again for me. Ever lead me to see that through Him I have forgiveness and an open heaven. Amen.

To Be a Good Missionary
Acts 11:7-9

Dear Father, I pray for all the boys and girls who do not know You. Help me lead them to Jesus. Let my life be a light to shine brightly in this world of sin. Hear me, in Jesus' name. Amen.

Dear Jesus, I am happy that You found me and are taking me to heaven. But many sinners have not yet come to You. Help me to seek the lost with Your Precious Gospel. Put the right words into my mouth and heart, and give me courage to say them. Help me to do many good works so that others may want to become Christians too. Amen.

For Understanding My Sunday School Lessons
Proverbs 2:1-9

Dearest Lord Jesus, help me to grow to be a better Christian. Help me to understand my Sunday school lessons well. Through them show me Your love and Your will for me, and make me more like You. Amen.

I confess that I need to study Your Word much more, dear God. Help me to live Your Word, understand it, remember it, and do it. Forgive me for not always being ready to listen. Make me happy to learn and study, to be a better child of God, to grow in wisdom and understanding, for Your name's sake. Amen.

To Trust His Promises
Proverbs 3:1-6

I am trusting Thee, Lord Jesus,
Never let me fall.
I am trusting Thee forever
And for all. Amen.

Lord God, You know all things and have promised me salvation and life with You in heaven. Give me a heart that trusts You fully. Send Your Holy Spirit to give me a strong faith when I read and hear Your promises. Take away all doubt and fear. Show me that You are the almighty God, who keeps His promises. Help me to believe with all my heart, for Jesus' sake. Amen.

For My Good Health
Psalm 139:1-18

Lord Jesus, above all things keep me always in Your love and, if it is Your will, also keep me in good health. Amen.

O God, You have given me a wonderful body, such as only You could make, and to this day You have kept me safe. You have kept me in good health when many things could have gone wrong. May I always be thankful for this. Don't let me use my body to do wrong. Make my soul strong and healthy by faith in the forgiveness of sins, and heal all who are sick. In Jesus' name I ask it. Amen.

To Be Kind
James 2:14-18

Heavenly Father, hear my thanks
For Your loving care;
Help me now to show my love,
And each blessing share. Amen.

On My Birthday
Psalm 100

Dear Jesus, today is my birthday. Because I am Your child, I know it will be a happy day. Be close to me all the time. As I grow older, help me also to grow more loving and kind. Give everyone a birthday as happy as mine. Amen.

Gracious Lord, You have let me come to the end of another year of my life. Your hand of love has blessed me. I don't deserve anything good, because I still sin every day. I thank You for forgiving me for Jesus' sake and pray that You will help me to start a new life in my next year. Let me be happy in doing Your will. Stay with me day by day, and help me to love You more all the time. If it is Your will, give me more happy birthdays, for Jesus' sake. Amen.

To Be Like Jesus
John 15:4-12

Jesus, Friend of little children, be a Friend to me.
Take my hand, and ever keep me close to Thee.
Teach me how to grow in goodness daily as I grow.
You have been a child, and surely You must know.
Amen.

Loving Father, Your Son Jesus was kind and good. He helped the sick and crippled, fed the hungry, and loved those who hated Him. He suffered and died for all sinners. Help me to be like Him—not selfish, hateful, mean. As He loved others, let me love them, too, because He first loved me. This I ask for His sake. Amen.

For Jesus' Love

1 John 4:10-16

Dear Lord God, You are good to me because You love me. I thank You for Your goodness. Be with me always with Your love. In Jesus' name I pray. Amen.

Without the love of Jesus, dear God, I cannot live. Without His love my sins would not be washed away. Without His love my home, my family, my friends, my church, and all my gifts could not save me. I believe Your promise that nothing shall separate me from the love of Jesus and from the love that You have for me in Him. Keep me in this glorious faith, through Christ Jesus, my Lord. Amen.

To Obey

Colossians 3:20-25

O God, through the holy obedience of Your Son, my Savior, make me willing to obey You, my parents, teachers, and all others whom You have placed over me in my life, for Jesus' sake. Amen.

Dear Father in heaven, I know that I have not always obeyed my father and mother, my teachers, and all whom You have placed over me. I have not always seen them as Your gifts to lead me to You. I

*Help me see Your hand and gift
in all that is beautiful.*

confess that wanting my own way gets me into trouble. Forgive these sins, I pray, and give me power to follow Your way even when it seems hard, through Jesus Christ, my Lord. Amen.

To Be a Good Neighbor
Luke 11:29-37

Lord, open wide my eyes to see
That love is needed everywhere,
And help I always ready be
My love with other folks to share. Amen.

Lord Jesus, how happy I am that You have given me good neighbors and playmates. I ask forgiveness for not always having treated them kindly. May I ever be friendly and forgiving, and never hurt others for hurting me. Help me to be well liked by showing Your love to all. Amen.

For Help With My Schoolwork
Matthew 25:14-30

Heavenly Father, help me to listen well and to understand my lessons. Help me to do my best and make good use of the mind You have given me. Bless my teachers, too. I pray in Jesus' name. Amen.

Heavenly Father, to be a good Christian, to be a good example to others, to be a good missionary, I need You every hour. Bless my going to school. Help me to understand the lessons I am taught and to learn them well. Make me willing to study, and forgive me when I haven't tried hard enough. Most of all, let me learn from You, for Jesus' sake. Amen.

When a New School Year Begins
Luke 2:40-52

Dear heavenly Father, I thank You for my school. Help me to go there gladly and do my best to learn what is taught. Help me be a better child of Yours. Bless the teachers and the work they do. In Jesus' name I ask it. Amen.

Dear Lord, Your mercy has permitted me to begin another year of study. I thank You for all the blessings of the past school years. Bless me as I study and learn about You. Give the teachers wisdom as they teach. Help all of us pupils to study hard and to live what we learn. Make us friendly, kind, and obedient. Cause us all, teachers and pupils, to win many souls for Jesus, who died to save us from our sins. In His name I ask it. Amen.

When Going on a Trip
Psalm 121

Thank You, dear Jesus, for being kind and good to me and my family. Forgive us our sins, and fill our hearts with love for You. Be with us wherever we go, and keep us safe and help us enjoy our trip. In You alone we trust. Amen.

Heavenly Father, I need You wherever I go. As I begin this trip, I ask for Your protection, that Your holy angels will keep me safe. Help me see Your hand and gift in all that is beautiful. Help me to sing Your praise wherever I am. Bring me safely home. Make me happy to be Your child, living in Your wonderful world, for Jesus' sake. Amen.

When on Vacation

Psalm 46

Dear Father in heaven, I thank You for my vacation, when I can have fun with my family and friends. Be with me, and keep me with You. Protect me from all harm, and make me ever joyful in Your goodness. In Jesus' name I pray. Amen.

I thank You, Lord, for giving me time for rest and play. Help me to use this time to see Your goodness in everything around me—the beautiful country, trees, flowers, animals, fresh air, and warm sunshine. Cause me to use my vacation time to rest and grow strong that I may go back to my regular work, study, and play more ready to live for You. Forgive me for not always being thankful for Your love. Hear me for Jesus' sake. Amen.

Thank You for my family and friends.

Color photos by Robert Mittelstaedt. Black-and-white photos by Hal. H. Harrison, Monkmeyer Press Photo Service; Luoma Photos; Savage Studios